JOSÉ DE SAN MARTÍN

LATIN AMERICA'S QUIET HERO

JOSÉ B. FERNANDEZ

Hispanic Heritage
The Millbrook Press
Brookfield, Connecticut

Facing page: Before cheering crowds, San Martín waves the flag in a newly freed Lima, Peru.

I wish to express my gratitude and deep appreciation
to Mrs. Kimberly J. Hillyard and Miss Karen L. Banks
for their invaluable comments and suggestions
in reading the manuscript. I am also indebted to
Commodore Adrián Speranza of the Argentine Air Force
for his assistance and contributions. Finally,
Frank Menchaca, my editor at The Millbrook Press,
deserves a special thanks for skillfully
guiding the project through all of its phases.

Library of Congress Cataloging-in-Publication Data
Fernandez, José B., 1948–
José de San Martín : Latin America's quiet hero / by José B.
Fernandez.
p.   cm.—(Hispanic heritage)
Includes bibliographical references (p.) and index.
Summary: A biography of the Argentinian general who was
instrumental in liberating South America from Spanish rule in the
early nineteenth century.
ISBN 1-56294-383-9 (lib. bdg.)
1. San Martín, José de, 1778–1850—Juvenile literature.   2. South
America—History—Wars of Independence, 1806–1830—Juvenile
literature.   3. Statesmen—South America—Biography—Juvenile
literature.   4. Generals—South America—Biography—Juvenile
literature.   [1. San Martín, José de, 1778–1850.   2. Generals.
3. South America—History—Wars of Independence, 1806–1830.]
I. Title.   II. Series.
F2235.4.F45   1994   980'.02'092—dc20   93-9735   CIP   AC

Map by Joe LeMonnier
Cover photograph courtesy of The Granger Collection
Photographs courtesy of the Organization of American States:
pp. 3, 20, 27, 29 (left); Bettmann Archive: pp. 4, 14, 20;
Superstock: p. 7; New York Public Library Picture Collection:
p. 8; National Maritime Museum, Greenwich, London: p. 13;
Author's collection: pp. 17, 19, 29 (right).

Published by The Millbrook Press
2 Old New Milford Road, Brookfield, Connecticut 06804

JOSÉ DE SAN MARTÍN

This painting shows San Martín, wrapped in a green cloak,
leading his men through the Andes.

The Andes Mountains of Latin America soar into the sky. They are the second-highest mountain range in the world. They divide the countries of Argentina and Chile.

In January 1817 an army of 5,200 men tried to do what no other army had ever done: cross the Andes from Argentina to Chile.

For days the army struggled up narrow mountain trails. Men had to walk in single file and hang on to one another. Many fell over cliffs. Some passed out from the thinness of the air. Others died from cold. At night the howling winds made the bravest soldiers tremble with fear.

But this army had a leader who feared neither the mountains nor the Spanish army that waited on the other side. He challenged both of them in order to free Latin America from Spanish rule. His name was José de San Martín.

THE BOY FROM YAPEYÚ · José Francisco de San Martín was born on February 25, 1778, in the village of Yapeyú, in what is today Argentina. Yapeyú sat on the bank of the Uruguay River. José had three older brothers and a younger sister. His father, Don Juan de San Martín, was an officer in the Spanish Army and the lieutenant governor of Yapeyú. His mother, Doña Gregoria Matorras, was also a Spaniard. (*Don* and *Doña* are names of respect given to men and women in Spanish).

Indian servants cared for the young José. They taught him Guarani, their language. Since Yapeyú was in a tropical forest, José used to see snakes and flamingos and other birds right from his front porch. He even saw large, fierce cats called jaguars. Sometimes, his Indian friends would take him to see the big crocodile-like caimans on the river. Little José stared at the caimans with his big, dark eyes. He did not say a word and never showed any fear.

The San Martín children loved living in Yapeyú. In 1781, however, Don Juan decided to move his family to Buenos Aires because he had not been paid in over three years.

Buenos Aires was at that time the capital of a region of Latin America controlled by Spain called the Viceroyalty of La Plata. The viceroyalty included what are today the countries of Argentina, Paraguay, and Uruguay. In Buenos Aires, José attended school, where he learned to read and write.

San Martín's
childhood
neighbors:
a jaguar
and
caimans.

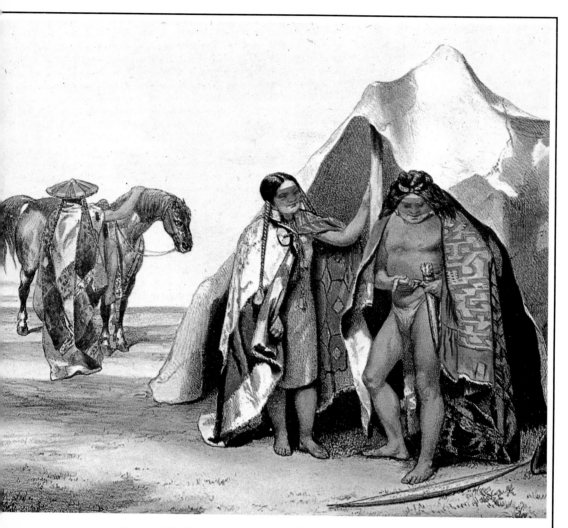

Guarani Indians in their traditional dress. Shown the
Guarani's way of life at a young age, San Martín understood
and respected this people.

THE GUARANI INDIANS

José de San Martín lived among the Guarani Indians until he was three years old. Over the years many Guarani died off due to disease. Today there are only a few left. They live in Paraguay and southern Brazil.

Most of the Guarani are dark and short. Guarani women wear white dresses with black and brown stripes. They are very good weavers. Guarani men wear clothes made of cotton. Their belts are made of human hair. The men paint their bodies. They make the paint from a tree called urucú (the annatto tree) or by mixing charcoal and honey. Many wear feather wreaths and rings they make of lizards' tails.

Guarani families live in houses made of palm trees. Guarani sleep in cotton hammocks or on straw mats.

Most Guarani Indians are farmers. They grow corn, beans, sweet potatoes, bananas, watermelons, and a tropical plant called manioc (cassava). The Guarani use manioc roots to make bread.

The Guarani are very good at hunting and fishing. Some fish with wooden hooks. Others shoot fish with bows and arrows that they make from palm trees.

The Guarani also hunt deer, monkeys, and animals called tapirs. The tapir is related to the rhinoceros but is much smaller. Unlike the rhinoceros, it has no horn and has a snout that looks like a chopped-off elephant trunk. Guarani children also hunt birds with blowguns and bamboo darts.

COLOMBIA

ECUADOR
Guayaquil

Amazon

BRAZIL

PERU

Lima

BOLIVIA

La Paz

PARAGUAY

Paraná

CHILE

Uruguay

ARGENTINA

URUGUAY

Santiago
Mendoza

Buenos Aires

PACIFIC
OCEAN

ATLANTIC
OCEAN

LATIN AMERICA DURING THE WAR FOR INDEPENDENCE

Viceroyalty of Peru

Viceroyalty of La Plata

Upper Peru

0   500 Miles

0   750 Kilometers

In 1785, when José was almost eight years old, Don Juan was promoted to colonel and ordered to go to Spain. He took his family with him.

LIFE IN SPAIN · José went to school in Madrid, the Spanish capital. At age eight he entered the Seminario de los Nobles, a boarding school for the sons of army officers and important Spaniards.

School was not easy. Students had to get up at five o'clock every morning and make their beds within ten minutes. They studied science, foreign languages, religion, music, drawing and mathematics, among other subjects. They also learned the art of sword fighting, called fencing, and hand-to-hand combat.

José was a fair student. His favorite subjects were mathematics and drawing, but he always had problems with writing. He got along very well with his classmates, though some found him to be too quiet.

When José turned twelve, he left the Seminario and joined the Army. He wanted to follow in his father's footsteps. He was admitted as a soldier-in-training, or cadet, to Spain's Murcia Regiment, whose colors were blue and white, José's favorites.

José's regiment was sent to North Africa in 1791 to help the defenders of a Spanish fort in Oran, Algeria. Pirates and warriors from Algeria and Morocco had attacked the fort. The Spaniards fought hard, but finally they surrendered. José was only thirteen when he was taken prisoner. A few months later he was allowed to return to Spain.

In 1796, Spain went to war against England. The English had taken Gibraltar, a Spanish territory, and Spain wanted it back. San Martín went to the Mediterranean Sea to fight on board the Spanish ship *Santa Dorotea*.

On July 15, 1798, the *Santa Dorotea* was attacked by the *Lion*, one of the most powerful ships in the British Navy. The *Lion* fired more than sixty-four cannon shots, blasting the *Santa Dorotea*'s masts and sails to pieces. The little Spanish ship fought until it ran out of ammunition. Eventually, the *Santa Dorotea*'s captain had to surrender, and San Martín once again became a prisoner.

Although he didn't enjoy being a prisoner on board the British ship, young San Martín made the best of a bad situation. He studied mathematics, improved his drawing skills, and learned to speak English. He also played checkers and chess with his British guards and beat them most of the time.

In 1800, San Martín and his fellow prisoners were freed. He rejoined his old Murcia Regiment. In March of 1808 the French emperor Napoleon Bonaparte invaded Spain. Napoleon had forced the Spanish king to step down and had named his brother Joseph as king. The

In this painting, the Lion *(left front) blasts the* Santa Dorotea *(right front), aboard which is San Martín.*

Spaniards refused to have a French king and rebelled. San Martín fought many battles for the Spanish.

In 1811, at the Battle of Albuera, San Martín put the fencing lessons he had had as a student to good use against a French officer. Their swords clanged for over an hour. Eventually, San Martín was wounded, and blood gushed from his hand. As the Frenchman approached to kill him, San Martín struck him with two sword thrusts to the body. The officer fell to the ground and died minutes later.

This painting by Spanish artist Francisco Goya shows French soldiers and Spanish people battling during Napoleon's invasion.

By late 1811 the French were on the run. Because of his skill as a soldier, San Martín was named commander of the Sagunto Regiment, one of the most famous regiments in the Spanish Army.

This, however, was his last command in the Spanish Army. The quiet officer from Yapeyú had spent twenty-two years of his life in that army. He had fought against the best soldiers of Europe. He had learned from them and even defeated some of them. He had earned the respect of his soldiers and proved himself to be a great leader. But now it was time to return to Argentina and fight for its freedom from Spain, the very country he had fought to defend.

"CAN I BE OF HELP?" · During the war with France, the Latin American colonies sided with Spain, even though Spain had never treated them very well. The Latin Americans, for example, were denied important jobs in their own government. They had to pay high taxes and had no freedom of speech. As a result, by 1811, many Latin Americans were ready to declare independence from Spanish rule. San Martín was among them.

On March 14, 1812, San Martín's ship landed in Buenos Aires. He went to see the leaders of the new Argentine Army fighting for independence. He announced: "Gentlemen, my name is José de San Martín. I am a soldier. Can I be of help?"

At first some of the leaders did not trust San Martín because he had been an officer in the Spanish Army. Some thought that he was a Spanish spy. After a long meeting, however, they decided to give him a chance. They made him a lieutenant colonel in their Army. His job was to train a cavalry regiment, a group of soldiers who fight on horseback.

San Martín gathered three hundred Indians from Yapeyú, where he had grown up, because he knew that they would make good soldiers. He also recruited gauchos—Argentine cowboys—because they were the best riders. Finally, he chose a group of young Creoles—people of Spanish background born in Latin America—because they were educated and he thought they could become good officers.

He spent much time training these men. As usual, he said little and let his dark eyes do the talking. He was tough with them, but fair. During the evenings, they listened to his stories about his days in the Spanish Army. His soldiers called him *El tío*—"Uncle"; he called them *mis muchachos*—"my boys."

One evening, San Martín went to a dance. There he met a beautiful young woman named Remedios Escalada. She was a very good dancer, and the quiet officer asked her to dance with him. She was much younger than he was, but that night he fell in love with Remedios. Five months later, on September 12, 1812, José and Remedios were married in Buenos Aires.

San Martín, however, had little time to spend with his wife. He had to keep training his men. By December 1812, San Martín's cavalry regiment—known as the Granaderos ("Grenadiers")—was ready to fight.

THE GRANADEROS

From 1813 until 1824, José de San Martín's Granaderos regiment fought in twenty major battles for Latin American independence. Nineteen generals and more than two thousand officers fought in the regiment. They won more medals than any other part of the army and helped free Argentina, Chile, Peru, Colombia, Ecuador, and Upper Peru. When the War for Independence was over, the regiment returned to Argentina. It broke up in 1826.

A Granadero in full uniform.

In 1903 the regiment was formed once again as part of the Argentine Army. In 1918 it was renamed Calvary Grenadier Regiment San Martín, in honor of its founder.

Today, the Granaderos are the official escorts of the Argentine president. They help to guard the Pink House—where the president of Argentina lives—and help to protect the president. Only the most qualified and best-disciplined soldiers can serve in this regiment. The Granaderos wear blue uniforms with wide white sashes, or shoulder bands, and carry sabers, or curved swords.

On January 28, 1813, San Martín set out from Buenos Aires with 120 grenadiers to attack the Spaniards. He had learned that the Spaniards were about to land soldiers near San Lorenzo, on the banks of the Paraná River.

On the evening of February 2, San Martín and his men arrived at San Lorenzo. The next day at dawn, San Martín climbed the tower of a nearby church. When he spotted three hundred Spanish soldiers about three hundred yards away, San Martín cried out *"¡Al ataque!"*— "Charge!"

San Martín mounted his horse and led his grenadiers. They surprised the Spaniards, who retreated. The grenadiers chased them, caught up, and fought the Spaniards in hand-to-hand combat.

The Spanish ships, anchored on the river, fired their cannons at the grenadiers. One of the shots killed San Martín's horse. The horse fell on San Martín's leg, pinning him to the ground. A Spanish soldier rushed up to kill him. Luckily, a grenadier named Baigorria stabbed the Spanish soldier. Another grenadier, Sergeant Juan Bautista Cabral, freed San Martín from under his dead horse.

The Spaniards retreated to their ships and sailed upriver. They left forty of their men dead as well as most of the army's equipment. San Martín was happy with the victory, but he was also saddened by the death of

In freeing San Martín, Juan Batista Cabral was stabbed, as shown in this poster. His last words were: "Don't worry about me. Only a few of us end our lives with strangers. Leave me. I die content having beaten the enemy. Long live our country!"

fifteen of his *muchachos*. Some even said he cried. The Battle of San Lorenzo was a great victory for San Martín, and it would not be his last one.

THE CROSSING OF THE ANDES · In 1814, San Martín was appointed commander of the Northern Army. He was ordered to attack the neighboring region controlled by the Spanish called the Viceroyalty of Peru. (The Viceroyalty of Peru comprised what are now the countries of Peru and Chile.) His orders said he had to invade Peru by way of a region called Upper Peru (which is now the country of Bolivia).

San Martín, shown in this painting, planned the crossing of the Andes for more than a year.

San Martín knew that the attack would be a failure because the Spanish troops in Upper Peru were too strong. He told his superiors that he was in poor health and quit as commander. He asked to be made governor of Argentina's Cuyo Province, next to the Andes mountains and across from Chile. His health, he explained, would improve in the clean mountain air. San Martín got his wish, but many people called him a coward.

Little did they know that San Martín was following his own secret plan. He wanted to raise an army in Cuyo and cross the Andes into Chile. Once Chile was free, he would move north and liberate Peru.

Since San Martín was always very quiet, his soldiers didn't know what was on his mind. In July 1816, however, San Martín addressed his officers: Gentlemen, my plan is to cross the Andes into Chile with this small but well-trained army. It's the only way to free Peru.

The officers couldn't believe what their commander was saying. One of them stood up and said: Sir, some of the Andes mountains are over 20,000 feet high. It's too risky. It is, simply, impossible.

San Martín's eyes blazed as he answered, Nothing is impossible as long as we are united.

Once his plan was announced, the people of Mendoza—the capital of Cuyo Province—began to help. Women sewed the soldiers' uniforms. Children went from door to door collecting blankets. Farmers began to gather corn for the army. Father Luis Beltrán, a local priest who knew science and mathematics, set up a factory. In the factory, he melted church bells to make guns, bullets, horseshoes, and swords. He also made canteens from cowhorns and even built portable bridges to carry the cannons across the mountains.

By January of 1817, San Martín had an army of 5,200 men. The army was made up of a wide variety of people. There were Creoles from Buenos Aires, gauchos from the plains of Argentina, Guarani Indians, Chileans, British volunteers, and black slaves that San Martín had freed.

On January 5, 1817, San Martín gathered his army for a parade. As the soldiers paraded through the streets of Mendoza, San Martín raised a light-blue-and-white flag which his wife, Remedios, had sewn and cried out: "Long live independence! This is the flag of independence! Do you swear to die in the defense of this flag?"

"We do," cried out the troops.

As San Martín made the final preparations for the crossing, a Spanish spy arrived in Santiago, Chile. He went to see General Marcó del Pont, the Spanish commander, and told him that San Martín was about to cross the Andes. Marcó del Pont thought it was impossible and did not pay attention to the spy's warning.

On the morning of January 19, 1817, an army of 5,200 men, 1,600 horses, and 10,000 mules left Mendoza for Chile. The mules carried ammunition and enough food to last for three weeks—San Martín's estimated crossing time. They also carried medical supplies, fire logs, and onions and garlic. At that time, people mistakenly thought that onions and garlic could fight off the dizziness and bleeding caused by the thinness of the air high in the mountains.

Crossing the Andes meant a difficult three-hundred-mile march. In the daytime, men had to guide mules through the steep mountain passes. Many soldiers had to walk barefoot over the rocky terrain because they had no shoes. Their feet were blistered and frozen. In the evenings, the soldiers huddled together to protect themselves from snowstorms. As the soldiers reached the top of the mountains, they began to suffer from *puna*—a type of mountain sickness—and many began to bleed from their ears and nostrils. San Martín himself suffered from arthritis, but nothing was going to stop him. He kept cheering his troops on as they struggled over the Andes.

On February 8, 1817, twenty-one days after it had left Mendoza, the tired but proud Army of the Andes reached the Chilean plains of Chacabuco. San Martín and his men had done the impossible.

News of San Martín's crossing reached Marcó del Pont in Santiago. But it was too late. On February 12, 1817, San Martín's soldiers fell like lions on the Spanish troops at Chacabuco and scored an important victory. The first step in the liberation of Chile had been completed.

Hat in hand, San Martín embraces Chilean general Bernardo O'Higgins in victory at Maipú.

ON TO LIBERATION · After the Battle of Chacabuco, the Spaniards fled southward. Before pursuing them, San Martín decided to raise money and continue training his army. A little more than a year later, the army was ready to drive the Spanish out of the rest of Chile.

On April 5, San Martín led his army in the Battle of Maipú, one of the bloodiest battles in the wars for Latin American independence. The Spanish soldiers charged bravely and furiously. Time after time they were beaten back by San Martín's soldiers. The Spaniards even sent in the famous Burgos Regiment, which had never lost a battle. The Burgos was about to break through San Martín's defenses when the Granaderos came to the rescue and the Spanish regiment retreated and eventually surrendered. When the battle ended, Chile was no longer a Spanish colony; it was a free country.

Now the liberation of Peru remained. No army could make it through the thousand-mile-long Atacama Desert, which separated Chile from Peru. The only way to invade Peru was by sea, but San Martín had no navy.

In November 1818, however, an English admiral, Lord Cochrane, landed in Chile and offered to help the patriots. In January 1819, Lord Cochrane began a year of raiding the Peruvian coast, capturing Spanish ships, getting supplies, and landing spies for the invasion.

Meanwhile, the Buenos Aires leaders wanted San Martín back in Argentina. Spain, they thought, was going to invade Argentina, and civil war was also breaking out in the Argentine provinces. San Martín was faced with one of the toughest decisions of his life. Should he be loyal to his country, or should he liberate Peru and, with it, Latin America? The quiet warrior thought and waited. When news arrived that the Spaniards could not launch an invasion of Argentina, he asked the leaders of Buenos Aires for permission to go ahead with the invasion of Peru. They denied it. San Martín decided to go ahead anyway and resigned from the Argentine Army.

A great uproar followed in Buenos Aires when the news of San Martín's decision reached that city. Some said it was a great act of disobedience. Others called him a traitor. These charges hurt him very much, but he never showed his hurt in public.

San Martín began landing men in Peru. Lord Cochrane's naval raids were also crippling the Spanish army. Meanwhile, support for the Spanish government in Peru was failing. More and more people—many of them Peruvian Indians and black slaves—were joining San Martín's army. Even some members of the Spanish army switched to San Martín's side.

On June 2, 1821, the Spanish governor of Peru agreed to leave Lima, Peru's capital. In July, San Martín's army entered the city without firing a shot. San Martín now held Lima, but the Spaniards still held much of Peru and outnumbered San Martín's army two to one.

The liberation of the rest of Latin America, however, was to be the fight of another man. His name was Simón Bolívar. He was a general from Venezuela who had freed his country along with Colombia and Ecuador.

In July 1822, San Martín went to Ecuador to meet Bolívar and to plan the liberation of Peru and the rest of Latin America together. But San Martín quickly saw that they were too different to work with each other. San Martín was quiet. He cared little for what others thought of him. Bolívar was emotional. He loved attention and

Latin America's two great liberators, San Martín (left) and Simón Bolívar, meet in Guayacil, Ecuador.

glory. Bolívar was a politician and San Martín was just a soldier. San Martín was afraid that their differences would hurt the cause of freedom in Latin America. There was room for only one leader.

A LONG REJECTION · After his meeting with Bolívar, San Martín made another big decision. He quietly withdrew from the Army and left the liberation of Latin

America up to Bolívar. On his way back to Buenos Aires, he heard that his wife, Remedios, was dying. He rushed to reach her before she died. But he had to stop along the way to avoid being attacked by bandits. She died before he could get to her. When Remedios died, San Martín told a friend: "I have not only lost my wife, but my best friend." San Martín was now alone but for his daughter, Mercedes.

When he finally returned to Buenos Aires he found he was rejected. The Argentine people, who had once called him a hero, now felt he had let them down by leaving the Army. He could not make them understand his reasons for doing so. San Martín left the country that he had risked everything to defend and went to live in Europe. He and Mercedes moved to Belgium.

In 1825, Simón Bolívar completed the liberation of Latin America. Without San Martín's work, he would not have succeeded. San Martín thought that maybe now his people would accept him. In 1829 he sailed to his homeland. His ship was not allowed to land. His people did not want him back.

San Martín went to France. He lived a quiet life, painting pictures and reading. As he put it, "learning never stops." When Mercedes married and had two children, San Martín learned toy making for his grandchildren. In 1850, José de San Martín died at age seventy-two. His last wish was to be buried in Argentina.

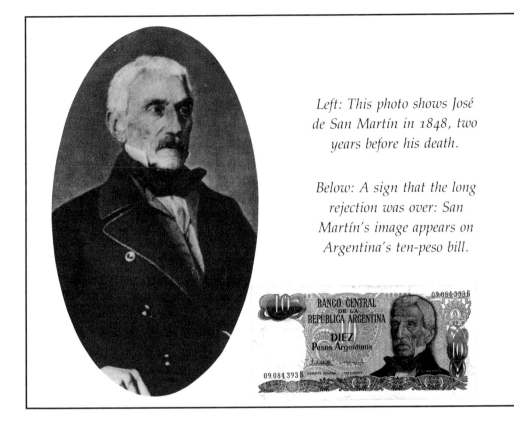

Left: This photo shows José de San Martín in 1848, two years before his death.

Below: A sign that the long rejection was over: San Martín's image appears on Argentina's ten-peso bill.

It took thirty years to make his wish come true. The Argentine people were slow to change their minds about him. In 1880, however, his body was moved from France to Argentina.

Today, many towns and cities in Latin America honor San Martín with statues and by naming streets after him. Almost all Latin American schoolchildren read about the life of the quiet warrior from Yapeyú.

IMPORTANT DATES IN THE LIFE OF JOSÉ DE SAN MARTÍN

1778   San Martín is born on February 25, in Yapeyú, Argentina.

1790   San Martín enters the Spanish Army.

1812   San Martín joins the Argentine Army and is made a lieutenant colonel. He forms the Granaderos regiment. He marries Remedios Escalada.

1813   San Martín defeats the Spaniards at the Battle of San Lorenzo, on February 3.

1816   San Martín is appointed commander in chief and captain general of the Army of the Andes.

1817   San Martín crosses the Andes Mountains with his army. He defeats the Spaniards at the Battle of Chacabuco, Chile, on February 12.

1818   San Martín wins the Battle of Maipú, the most important battle for Chilean independence, on April 5.

1819   San Martín resigns from the Argentine Army and plans to go ahead with the liberation of Peru.

1821   San Martín captures Lima, Peru's capital, on June 2.

1822   San Martín meets with Simón Bolívar in Guayaquil, Ecuador; he retires and leaves the liberation of Latin America up to Bolívar. His wife, Remedios, dies.

1824   San Martín leaves for Europe with his daughter, Mercedes.

1850   José de San Martín dies in Bolougne-Sur-Mer, France, on August 17.

FIND OUT MORE
ABOUT JOSÉ DE SAN MARTÍN

———————————————■———————————————

San Martin: Knight of the Andes by Ricardo Rojas. Translated by Herschel Brickell and Carlos Videla. New York: Cooper Square Publishers, 1967.

San Martin: The Liberator by J.C.J. Metford. Westport, Conn.: Greenwood Press, 1971.

ABOUT ARGENTINA AND SOUTH AMERICA

———————————————■———————————————

Argentina by Karen Jacobsen. Chicago: Childrens Press, 1990.

The Land & People of Argentina by Geoffrey Fox. New York: HarperCollins, 1989.

Living in South America by Chantal Henry-Biabaud. Ossining, N.Y.: Young Discovery Library, 1991.

South America by D. V. Georges. Chicago: Childrens Press, 1986.

South America by Francene Sabin. Mahwah, N.J.: Troll Associates, 1985.

Take a Trip to Argentina by Keith Lye. New York: Franklin Watts, 1986.

INDEX

Page numbers in *italics* refer to illustrations.